OIL SPILL!

DISASTER IN THE GULF OF MEXICO

ELAINE LANDAU

M
MILLBROOK PRESS
MINNEAPOLIS

Millbrook Press
A division of Lerner Publishing Group, Inc.
241 First Avenue North
Minneapolis, MN 55401 U.S.A.

Website address: www.lernerbooks.com

Library of Congress Cataloging-In-Publication Data

Landau, Elaine.
    Oil spill! : disaster in the Gulf of Mexico / by
Elaine Landau.
      p.   cm.
    Includes bibliographical references and index.
    ISBN: 978–0–7613–7485–5 (lib. bdg. : alk.
paper)
    1. BP Deepwater Horizon Explosion and Oil
Spill, 2010—Juvenile literature. 2. Oil spills—
Mexico, Gulf of—Juvenile literature. I. Title.
GC1221.L36 2011
363.738'20916364—dc22   2010029390

Manufactured in the United States of America
1 – DP – 12/31/10

Firefighting boats battle flames on the
Deepwater Horizon drilling rig on April 21, 2010.

CONTENTS

CHAPTER 1
APRIL 20, 2010

THE DAY STARTED OUT WELL FOR THE CREW ON THE DEEPWATER HORIZON OIL RIG. They had nearly finished drilling an oil well in the Gulf of Mexico, about 50 miles (80 kilometers) from the Louisiana coast. And that morning, the crew had received a visit from officials of the energy company that would use the well. They came to honor the 126 men and women on board for their strong safety record.

Working on an oil rig can be dangerous. The crew of the Deepwater Horizon was drilling a well through the ocean floor under 5,000 feet (1,524 meters) of water. The pressure at that depth is very high. That means the risk of explosions is also high. Yet no one expected anything to go wrong. The Deepwater Horizon had drilled wells under great depths before.

But at about a quarter to ten that night, the crew knew they were in trouble. First, a hissing sound filled the air.

The Deepwater Horizon oil rig was longer and wider than a football field. It held all the machines needed to drill a well deep through the ocean floor.

It was the sound of gas spewing onto the rig. The gas had shot up from the well through a pipe connected to the rig. Soon the rig's engines began to race. They were taking in the escaping gas.

Gas had escaped from the well before. Small amounts had come up since the drilling began earlier that year. But this was different. Much more gas was escaping. And it was rising with deadly speed and force.

Suddenly, a thundering boom pierced the air as the gas caught fire and exploded. More explosions followed. They rocked the rig. A 3-inch-thick (8-centimeter) steel door flew off its hinges. The hallway turned into a fiery path. The force of the blasts tossed full-grown men into the air. Later, one crew member recalled, "We were all sure we were going to die."

AN OFFSHORE DRILLING RIG

rig
(not drawn
to scale)

sea level

riser —
(pipe)

ocean

blowout
preventer

ocean floor

An offshore oil rig sits
above a well it drilled
through the ocean floor.
The well reaches oil
deep underground.

well —

oil

How could this have happened? The surge of gas and mud should have been stopped by the rig's blowout preventer. That was a 450-ton (408-metric-ton) safety device that sat on the ocean floor. Valves (parts that allow or prevent flow) inside the device should have stopped gas from escaping and blowing up the rig. But the Deepwater Horizon's blowout preventer had been having problems. At the crucial moment on April 20, it failed.

The crew scrambled to get to the rig's four lifeboats. They found that two of the boats had blown off the rig. Some people panicked. They jumped into the sea. It was slick with oil spilling from the rig. Others made it to the two remaining lifeboats.

By then the oil rig had turned into a fireball. Flames shot more than 150 feet (46 m) into the air. Those in the lifeboats had to escape the raging fire. They headed for the *Damon B. Bankston*, a nearby ship at sea. When the lifeboats made it to the ship, seventeen injured men were unloaded first. Eleven crew members never reached safety. They were killed in the disaster.

For two days, firefighting boats tried to control the flames on the Deepwater Horizon. But on April 22, the rig sank. Yet that was not the end of the disaster. A second tragedy was just beginning to unfold. As the rig's drilling platform fell into the sea, the pipe, called a riser, leading to the well went with it. The riser was left crumpled and leaking in several places on the ocean floor.

The oil leaking from the pipe was thick and smelly. Much of it floated up to the water's surface. By about ten days after the accident, the oil filled an area of nearly 3,850 square miles (9,971 sq. km). That's about twice the size of Delaware.

Firefighting boats try to put out the flames the day after the explosion on the Deepwater Horizon.

THE BLOWOUT PREVENTER

After the burst of gas from the well, the blind shear rams within the blowout preventer should have pinched the drill pipe closed and sliced it off. But it didn't work properly.

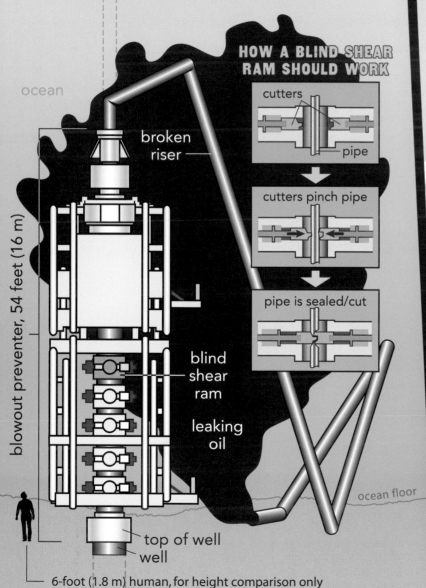

ocean

HOW A BLIND SHEAR RAM SHOULD WORK

broken riser

cutters

pipe

cutters pinch pipe

pipe is sealed/cut

blowout preventer, 54 feet (16 m)

blind shear ram

leaking oil

ocean floor

top of well

well

6-foot (1.8 m) human, for height comparison only

People knew wind and water currents could carry the oil to shorelines. Thousands of workers helped with cleanup efforts on the water. The government stepped in to take charge. But scientists figured that about 5,000 barrels (210,000 gallons, or 794,937 liters) of oil continued to escape from the well each day. They would later realize it was even more than that.

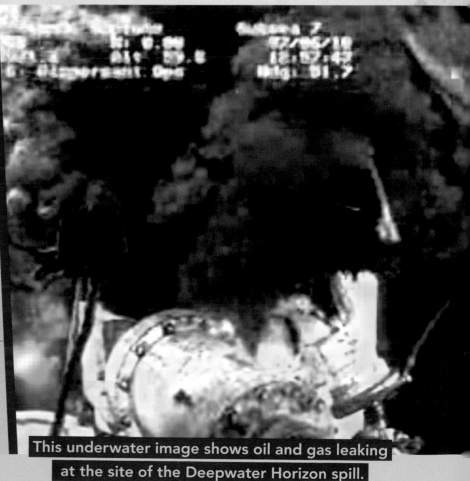

This underwater image shows oil and gas leaking at the site of the Deepwater Horizon spill.

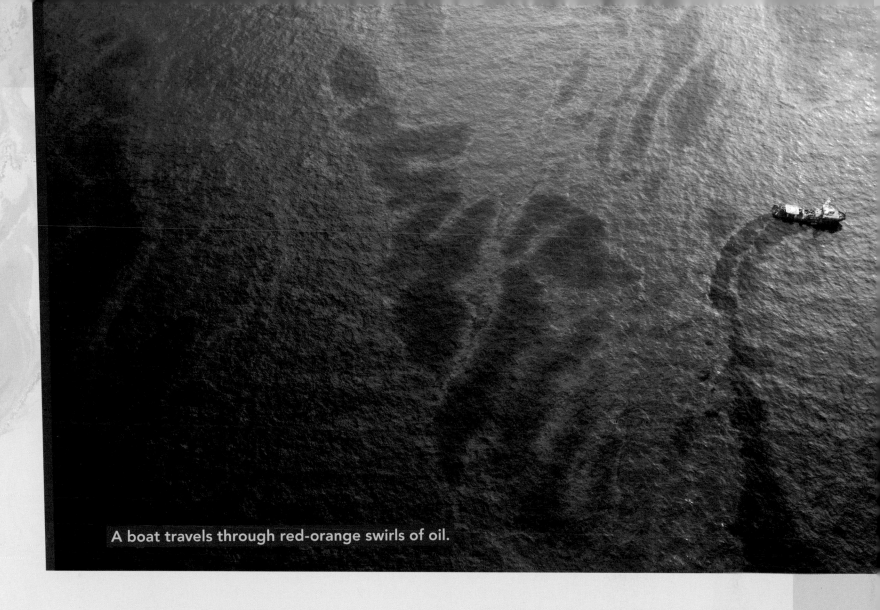

A boat travels through red-orange swirls of oil.

Something had to be done to stop the oil leak. And there was no time to waste. Mary Landry, U.S. Coast Guard rear admiral, sensed the urgency on April 28. "If we don't secure the well, this could be one of the most significant spills in U.S. history," she reported.

CHAPTER 2
STOPPING THE LEAK

THE OIL COMPANY BRITISH PETROLEUM, OR BP, WAS IN CHARGE OF CLOSING UP THE WELL. BP is one of the world's five largest energy companies. It had operated the Deepwater Horizon rig. So BP was responsible for the damage.

Stopping the oil flow was not going to be easy. The oil rig's blowout happened at a depth of 5,000 feet (1,524 m). The pressure there is so great that it would crush human divers. Remote-controlled robots had to be used to reach the ocean floor.

On April 25, BP sent down robots to close a valve on the blowout preventer. This valve should have automatically closed off the oil well and sliced off the drill pipe after the drilling platform exploded. That would have kept more oil from flowing into the ocean. But the valve hadn't closed. And the robots couldn't fix it. Oil continued to leak.

Leaders at BP believed drilling relief wells would be the best long-term solution. They would close off the leaking well by drilling a new well into it. A heavy fluid known as drilling mud would be shot into the leaking well through the relief well. The pressure from the mud's weight would stop the oil's flow. Then cement would be poured in to seal it off. Two relief wells would be drilled in case the first missed the mark. Workers began drilling the relief wells on May 2. But drilling on the ocean floor takes time. The wells would not be completed before August, at the earliest.

Meanwhile, BP had to try something else to contain the leak. So on May 7, the robots were sent down again. This time they lowered a large dome toward the leak to catch the oil. The oil would be pumped out of the dome to a ship at the surface.

But the dome had problems right away. Temperatures far below sea level are very cold. As the dome was lowered, icy crystals formed on the inside.

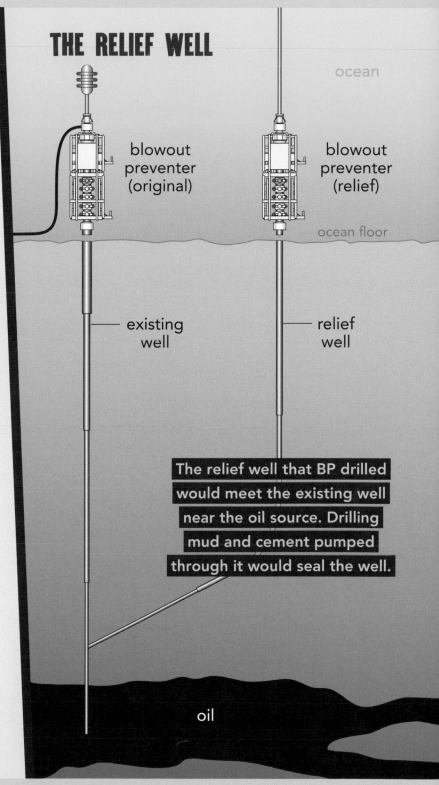

THE RELIEF WELL

ocean

blowout preventer (original)

blowout preventer (relief)

ocean floor

existing well

relief well

The relief well that BP drilled would meet the existing well near the oil source. Drilling mud and cement pumped through it would seal the well.

oil

They clogged it. This blocked the oil's way out. So the dome was set aside on the ocean floor while new plans took shape.

On May 16, a narrow tube was stuck into the damaged riser. A long pipe was connected to the 5-foot (1.5 m) tube. It carried the oil to a ship at the surface. The tube was able to catch more than 2,000 barrels (84,000 gallons, or 318,000 liters) of the leaking oil each day.

But BP's engineers were already working on their next plan to plug the well. They removed the tube after nine days. Then drilling mud was pumped down the pipe from the surface. Hoses attached to the blowout preventer carried the mud into the well. Officials hoped the heavy mud would stop the oil flow. But this "top kill" wasn't enough. BP also tried a "junk shot," clogging the blowout preventer with golf balls, shredded tires, and other objects. But this "shot" at stopping the leak failed too.

In early June, BP used remote-controlled robots with huge scissors to slice off most of the damaged riser. Then a cap was loosely fitted on top of the remaining pipe. Engineers had designed this cap so that ice wouldn't build up inside. A new pipe attached to the cap acted like a giant straw. It sucked up the oil to a ship at the surface.

This method worked fairly well. But it didn't collect all the oil. And in bad weather on July 2, the cap bounced around in the water. Oil slipped past it. Enough oil escaped to fill an Olympic-sized swimming pool.

By mid-July, things had begun to turn a corner. A new tightly fitting cap replaced the loosely fitting cap on the well. For the first time since the

The containment cap fits loosely on top of the riser.

oil spill began, the leak into the Gulf stopped. U.S. government scientists determined that 4.1 million barrels (172 million gallons, or 652 million liters) of oil had leaked into the ocean since the Deepwater Horizon rig sank. Others thought the amount was between 3 million and 5.2 million barrels (126 to 218 million gallons, or 477 to 827 million liters). No one could be absolutely sure. But finally, no new oil was escaping.

With the cap preventing any leaks, plugging the well underground would be easier. So on August 3, BP began the

The new cap is lowered into position in July.

"static kill." About 2,300 barrels (96,600 gallons, or 365,700 liters) of drilling mud were poured into the well through hoses. This was followed by cement. The mud and cement pushed the oil back into the reservoir. They sealed the well under the ocean floor. The relief wells would make sure the well was sealed for good.

By September, the first relief well had almost reached the oil well. Crews put extra safety devices in place over the oil well. The drilling crew then carefully drilled the relief well into exactly the right spot. About 18,000 feet (5,486 m) below the water's surface, the relief well met the 7-inch-wide (18 cm) oil well.

The crew pumped cement through the new well. As planned, it plugged the oil well at the very bottom. On September 19, 2010, the world got the news it had been waiting for. Thad Allen, the leader of the U.S. response to the oil spill, announced that the well was finally dead.

CHAPTER 3
THE CLEANUP

WHILE SCIENTISTS AND ENGINEERS WORKED ON STOPPING THE OIL LEAK, EFFORTS TO CLEAN UP THE OILY MESS WERE ALREADY UNDER WAY. Soon after the oil rig sank, BP began using dispersants to fight the oil spill. These chemicals break down oil into smaller drops. Then bacteria (microscopic living things) in the water can eat most of the oil drops.

Scientists counted on bacteria to get rid of much of the spilled oil. So they poured many gallons of dispersants on the surface oil. They also used dispersants deep in the ocean, near the leak. But dispersants had never been used at that depth before. Some people became concerned. They worried how the chemicals might affect deep-sea life. They argued that the dispersant BP was using, Corexit, was too harmful to the environment. The Environmental Protection Agency (EPA) agreed. It ordered BP to cut back on using Corexit. Still, a total of nearly 2 million gallons (7.5 million liters) of dispersants had gone into the Gulf by August.

A plane sprays oil dispersants into the Gulf.

Skimming boats quickly joined the fight against the oil spill. These boats skim oil from the water's surface. Special belts, brushes, or other machines separate the oil from the water. They pick up the oil and leave the cleaned water behind. Then barges collect the oil from the skimming boats. Skimmers patrolled the Gulf for months. But they work best in calm waters. The Gulf's waters were often too choppy for them.

Cleanup crews also used booms to contain the surface oil. Booms are long pieces of plastic. The top of the booms floats on the water. Their skirtlike bottom hangs down several inches. Booms were placed along beaches to stop oil from washing up on the shore. Millions of feet of booms were stretched across the Gulf's coasts.

LEFT: Booms are placed to trap oil before the spill reaches the coast of Louisiana.

BELOW: A boat skims oil from the water's surface.

Berms, or mounds of sand, 10 feet (3 m) tall line a beach in Alabama.

For booms to work well, people must carefully track the flow of oil. Then ships or beach crews can move the booms to where they are most needed. Yet this did not always happen in the Gulf. In addition, calm water is needed for booms to do their job. Rough water can send oil over or under booms.

Booms can't contain oil beneath the surface. So off the Louisiana coastline, berms were built to keep out the oil. Berms are human-made mounds of sand, built upward from the ocean floor. Oil can't flow under a berm. In July berms kept large amounts of oil from reaching land.

But the berms raised concerns. They often don't hold up well in storms. Building berms also requires dredging, or digging, of the ocean floor. That's where the extra sand comes from. Scientists say this could harm the environment and cause problems in the future.

Some of the oil on the water's surface was burned off. These controlled burns slowed the oil's spread. Yet at times, wind and rough seas made this method impossible. The controlled burns also posed a danger to animals such as sea turtles and whales. They could become trapped in the fires.

Oil spill expert Richard Charter, from the group Defenders of Wildlife, was well aware of the lack of good options. "In a spill this large, constantly fed by fresh oil, there are no easy answers," he noted. "There are only ranges of risks."

Scientists think most of the oil spill cleanup will happen through nature, not people. Oil at the surface is broken up by waves. It evaporates into the air. Oil slowly breaks down in the water, and bacteria eat it. But this will take a long time, especially in deep water. The bacteria living there eat the oil very slowly.

The U.S. government reported in August 2010 that about three-fourths of the spilled oil was already cleaned up. It said the oil had been removed naturally and by skimming, burning, and other efforts.

But some scientists had doubts. Science professor Robert Carney studies the oceans at Louisiana State University. He argued that it's "exceedingly hard" to know where oil spreads. Scientists needed a better idea of how much total oil had spilled and how much was still hidden in deep water or sand. What they did know was that the cleanup would go on for years.

A boat watches over a controlled burn in the Gulf.

CHAPTER 4
DISASTROUS EFFECTS

OIL SPILLS ARE UGLY. They are also harmful to living things. The United States has weathered oil spills in the past. But it never had to deal with a spill of this size.

The oil didn't take long to spread. It soon washed up on the shores of Louisiana, Mississippi, and Alabama. Then it hit some of Florida's white sandy beaches. By early July, tar balls—small, sticky balls of oil—were spotted in Texas. That meant the spill had affected all five states in the Gulf Coast.

Soiled shorelines weren't the only problem. When oil spills at the surface or in shallow water, it floats. The oil pollutes the water. It can kill seabirds, fish, shrimp, and other sea creatures. The Gulf oil spill was especially dangerous. Huge patches of oil were discovered at very low depths of the sea.

A brown pelican covered in oil sits on a beach.

Sharks and squid live in these deep regions. Marlins, snappers, and groupers swim there too. Deep-sea corals and jellyfish live on or near the seafloor as well. These creatures would be safe from an oil slick on the water's surface. But deep oil may put them at risk.

Marine mammals, such as dolphins and whales, are affected too. The oil kills or gets into the fish they eat. Marine mammals also cannot survive without coming to the ocean's surface for air. But in the middle of an oil slick, they breathe in the oil.

The oil spill has taken a toll on seabirds. Brown pelicans in the area have been soaked with oil. The oil gets into the bird's throat and stomach. It sticks to its feathers. An oil-coated bird cannot fly or care for its young. Many die as a result of oil spills.

Sea turtles are at risk as well. Some of these turtle species are endangered (at risk of dying out forever). The sea turtles may eat poisonous globs of oil. They mistake them for jellyfish. Or they may crawl through oil to reach the shore, where they lay eggs. Some turtles died when they got caught in controlled burns on the water's surface. They were unable to escape in time.

A sea turtle swims in oily water.

Dolphins come to the surface in polluted water near Louisiana.

The oil spill was especially hard on baby turtles. Hatchlings struggle to swim through the oil. Oil on the beach can also harm them as they crawl toward water.

Oil threatened the Gulf Coast's wetland areas. These are swamps, marshes, islands, and forests that are often covered in shallow water. Many types of birds, fish, and other animals nest and breed there. In some cases, their young get their start in the wetlands.

BP tried to keep spilled oil from reaching wetlands. But the oil spread too quickly. Oil destroys wetlands. It coats the animals and plant life there. An oil-soaked animal has trouble breathing and eating. Some wetland animals are poisoned after eating other oil-covered or poisoned animals. Others starve because the oil has killed off their food source. The same thing happens to animals in the ocean. But the effect is especially harmful in wetlands because they are important breeding and nesting areas.

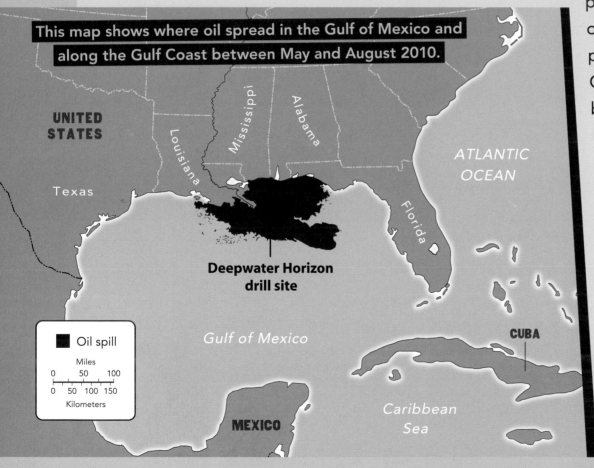

This map shows where oil spread in the Gulf of Mexico and along the Gulf Coast between May and August 2010.

UNITED STATES

Mississippi

Alabama

Louisiana

ATLANTIC OCEAN

Texas

Florida

Deepwater Horizon drill site

Oil spill

Miles
0   50   100

0 50 100 150
Kilometers

Gulf of Mexico

CUBA

MEXICO

Caribbean Sea

LEFT: A dragonfly sticks to oily marsh grass.
RIGHT: Oil coats the grass in an area where nothing kept the oil from coming ashore.

Wetlands are fragile. Plant life holds them together. Cleaning the water and the plants after an oil spill isn't easy. Scientists considered cutting away oil-covered plants or burning off the surface oil. But they found no perfect solution for wetlands.

The oil spill had disastrous effects on the people living in the Gulf. Many had made their living on the water. But with seafood polluted, suddenly shrimpers, oyster farmers, boat captains, and others were out of work. Some lost their businesses or homes because they couldn't pay the bills. Many believed their whole way of life was in danger.

Mark Jones Sr., an out-of-work shrimper, described the overall feeling. "I don't know what we can do," he said. "Our heritage is being washed away."

The oil spill also hurt tourism. Swimmers don't flock to oil-stained beaches. During the summer, many popular Gulf hotels were nearly empty.

The Gulf region needed help. BP set aside money to help people who had lost their jobs or were hurt by the oil spill in other ways. But for many residents, the money was not enough. The recovery of the Gulf Coast would be a long work in progress.

CHAPTER 5
WHAT'S TO BE DONE?

AS THE GULF OIL SPILL GREW IN APRIL, THE U.S. GOVERNMENT STEPPED IN TO HELP BP. President Barack Obama promised his commitment to end the disaster. "We're . . . using every resource available to stop the oil from coming ashore and [limit] the damage it could cause," he told people in the Gulf. National Guard members were sent to help with the cleanup.

President Obama also formed a National Response Team to handle the disaster. The team was made up of people from sixteen government departments and agencies. It helped BP create a plan to stop the oil leak. The team also worked on a plan to better protect coastal environments.

In addition, Obama directed the U.S. Navy secretary, Ray Mabus, to develop a long-term Gulf Coast Restoration Support Plan. Mabus held meetings with local people to hear their ideas. State and local governments worked on long-term recovery plans too.

A National Guard member sets up barriers to keep oil from washing onto the beach.

ABOVE: Rescue center workers clean oil off a brown pelican. RIGHT: Cleanup crews collect oil-covered debris.

Meanwhile, many volunteers pitched in daily to help the coast recover. They helped with beach cleanup. People who own boats helped on the water.

Other volunteers cleaned oil-soaked animals. Dozens of brown pelicans had been cleaned by early July. Making these birds ready for water again was hard. Their feathers had to be completely free of oil. When the animals were healthy, they were returned to clean areas of the wild.

The volunteers who flocked to the Gulf helped a lot. Yet they were only part of a broader solution. An important question lingered: how can we stop this from happening again?

People throughout the United States demanded change. Some took part in a protest called Hands across the Sand. On June 26, 2010, people stood hand in hand on beaches around the country. They wanted their lawmakers to make changes to better protect the environment.

On a beach in Mississippi, people hold hands during a Hands across the Sand event.

Logan Westerfield was one of hundreds of people who had gathered at a Florida beach that day. He expressed the concern that many Gulf residents felt. "The Gulf of Mexico is basically dying in front of us," he said.

Many people agree that we need change. Change could take many forms. It could mean less offshore drilling in the future. President Obama has stressed that the nation is too dependent on oil. Oil can hurt the environment. It takes millions of years to form underground. And we are quickly using up Earth's supply. President Obama believes other forms of energy should be explored. We may be able to get more energy from renewable sources. Renewable energy comes from natural resources that are quickly replaced. These include wind, sunlight, and heat from within Earth (which produces a type of energy called geothermal energy). But some people think renewable sources can't offer enough energy to be worthwhile.

Change could also mean more monitoring of offshore drilling. Equipment needs to be in tip-top shape. And safety must come first. This is important for both the workers and the environment. A reminder of this came on September 2, 2010. Just five months after the Deepwater Horizon explosion, another offshore rig in the Gulf of Mexico caught fire. No one was killed, and the wells under the rig were closed immediately. They didn't leak oil. But for many people, the fire was another example of the danger in offshore drilling. By late September, government officials announced several new safety rules. The rules set stricter guidelines for drilling, plugging wells, and monitoring blowout preventers. They also required oil companies to create plans to keep workers and the environment safe in any situation.

People everywhere can help bring change in another way—by using less energy and fewer natural resources. Everyone uses natural resources such as oil. But the less energy we use, the less oil we'll need for fuel and power. And less drilling for oil reduces the chances of an oil spill.

The Gulf of Mexico oil spill raised important questions about energy resources. Can the safety of offshore drilling be improved? Is drilling worth the risks? What other options do we have? Scientists, government leaders, and others weighed these questions after the 2010 disaster. The answers can't come soon enough.

Oil is a vital natural resource. So is the ocean water that covers offshore oil wells. We must respect our natural resources and use them wisely. This can go a long way toward preventing future disasters like the Gulf of Mexico oil spill.

WHAT YOU CAN DO

Want to do something about the Gulf oil spill? Young people can help in many ways. Here are just a few ideas for you to try:

1. Write to your representatives in Congress. (Visit the website http://www.congress.org/congressorg/directory/congdir.tt to find out who they are and where to reach them.) Tell them how you feel about the oil spill. Ask them to support renewable forms of energy. See if your friends will write letters too. Tell your teacher about it. Maybe it could be a class project.

2. Raise money to help Gulf wildlife. You could hold a bake sale. Ask local bakeries to donate baked goods. Ask your friends and neighbors to bake and help with the sale too. Send the money you make to a responsible wildlife group. Many are helping birds and turtles in the Gulf region. A parent, a teacher, or a librarian can help you find a good organization.

3. Help your family get "greener." Talk to your family members about how everyone can save more energy at home. Here are some ways to get started:

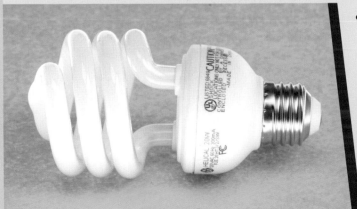

- Replace incandescent lightbulbs with compact fluorescent (CFL) lightbulbs. These are much more energy efficient, and they last longer.

- When you leave a room, turn off the lights. Be sure to turn off the computer and the TV too.

- In the winter, don't turn the heat up. Put on a warm sweater instead. You'll be saving energy.

- Don't ask your parents to drive you everywhere. Whenever possible, walk, bike, or take the bus.

- Take shorter showers. It doesn't take that long to get really clean. And run the dishwasher only when it's full. When you save water, you save energy.

- Recycle cans, bottles, and magazines. Your old notebook paper can be recycled too. The same goes for your computer paper and index cards. Do you know what would happen if all Americans recycled their newspapers once a week? Thirty-six million trees would be saved every year. How great for the environment!

OIL'S MESSY HISTORY

The 2010 oil spill in the Gulf of Mexico was not the first one. Huge tankers and supertankers (ships) carry oil all over the world. Over time, oil spills from tankers and offshore wells have created disasters in many different places. Here are some of the most notable spills in history.

The wreck of the *Torrey Canyon*

TORREY CANYON: MARCH 18, 1967

The supertanker *Torrey Canyon* crashed into a rocky reef (ridge) off the southwestern shore of England. About 35 million gallons (132 million liters) of oil spilled. Some was dispersed, skimmed, or burned. But oil washed up along 100 miles (161 km) of England's coast and 60 miles (97 km) of French coastlines.

IXTOC I: JUNE 3, 1979

The well Ixtoc I had a blowout in the Gulf of Mexico. It took about ten months to cap this well, which spilled nearly 140 million gallons (530 million liters) of oil. Currents carried the oil as far north as Texas. It killed fish, turtles, and seabirds along the way. In surveying the damage, scientists found shrimp with tumors in their tissues and crabs without pincers.

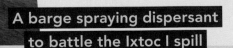

A barge spraying dispersant to battle the Ixtoc I spill

ATLANTIC EMPRESS AND AEGEAN CAPTAIN: JULY 19, 1979

Two large tankers, the *Atlantic Empress* and the *Aegean Captain*, collided near Tobago in the Caribbean Sea. Nearly 90 million gallons (341 million liters) of crude oil spilled. The collision also caused a fire that took firefighters more than two weeks to put out.

EXXON VALDEZ: MARCH 24, 1989

The tanker *Exxon Valdez* spilled more than 10 million gallons (42 million liters) of oil into Prince William Sound, Alaska. The environmental effects of that spill continue. Hundreds of thousands of birds and marine animals were killed, and many of those species still haven't recovered.

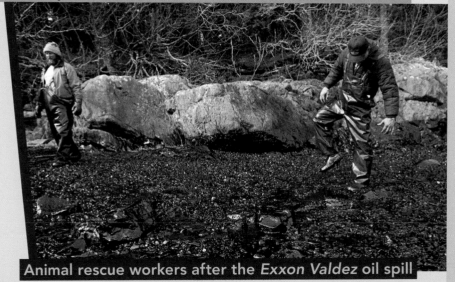

Animal rescue workers after the *Exxon Valdez* oil spill

GULF WAR OIL SPILLS: JANUARY 21, 1991

During the Gulf War (1991), Iraqi forces opened up oil wells and pipelines in Kuwait. Experts think that about 336 million gallons (1.3 billion liters) of oil were released into the Persian Gulf. This spilling of oil is considered the worst act of environmental warfare in history.

GLOSSARY

barge: a large flat-bottomed boat used to collect oil from vessels that skim it off the water's surface

berm: a large sand barrier built to protect the shoreline from oil

boom: a long piece of plastic placed along beaches or floated in the water to prevent oil from spreading past it

dispersant: a chemical used to break down oil particles

dredging: scooping out or removing material from beneath the water's surface

Environmental Protection Agency (EPA): a government agency with the task of protecting human health and the environment

geothermal energy: energy that comes from the heat inside Earth

hatchling: an animal that recently hatched from an egg

renewable energy: an energy source that can be replaced quickly by natural processes

skimmer: a boat used to skim oil from the water's surface

tourism: business from people visiting an area

wetland: a low area where the land is wet and soggy and often covered with shallow water

SOURCE NOTES

5   Ian Urbina and Justin Gillis, "Workers on Oil Rig Recall a Terrible Night of Blasts," *New York Times*, May 7, 2010, A1.

9   Ian Graham, "Oil Spill Update: Fire 'a Tool in the Toolkit,'" DoD Live, April 28, 2010, http://www.dodlive.mil/index.php/tag/rear-adm-mary-landry/ (August 19, 2010).

17 Brian Walsh, "The Spreading Stain," *Time*, July 21, 2010, 57.

17 Christine Dell'Amore, "Much Gulf Oil Remains, Deeply Hidden and under Beaches," *National Geographic News*, August 5, 2010, http://news.nationalgeographic.com/news/2010/08/100805-gulf-oil-spill-cement-static-kill-bp-science-environment/ (August 25, 2010).

21 Robert Samuels, "Gulf Oil Spill's Mental Toll Takes a Solemn Turn," *Miami Herald*, June 28, 2010, A1.

22 Mark Halperin, "Remarks: Obama on the Oil Spill," *Time*, May 2, 2010, http://thepage.time.com/remarks-obama-on-the-oil-spill-may-2-2010/ (September 2, 2010).

24 Luis Perez, "Drawing a Line in the Sand," *St. Petersburg Times*, June 27, 2010, 1B.

FURTHER READING AND WEBSITES

Beech, Linda Ward. *The Exxon Valdez's Deadly Oil Spill*. New York: Bearport, 2007.

Berkes, Marianne. *Marsh Morning*. Minneapolis: Millbrook Press, 2003.

EIA Energy Kids—Oil (Petroleum)
http://www.eia.doe.gov/kids/energy.cfm?page=oil_home-basics

Farden, John. *Oil*. London: DK, 2007.

Fleisher, Paul. *Ocean Food Webs*. Minneapolis: Lerner Publications Company, 2008.

Fridell, Ron. *Earth-Friendly Energy*. Minneapolis: Lerner Publications Company, 2009.

How You Can Help Wildlife Impacted by the BP Oil Spill
http://www.nwf.org/Oil-Spill.aspx

Johnson, Rebecca L. *A Journey into a Wetland*. Minneapolis: Lerner Publications Company, 2004.

Knight, M. J. *Why Should I Switch Off the Light?* Mankato, MN: Smart Apple Media, 2009.

OLogy—Marine Biology: The Living Oceans
http://www.amnh.org/ology/?channel=marinebiology

Storad, Conrad J. *Fossil Fuels*. Minneapolis: Lerner Publications Company, 2008.

Woods, Michael, and Mary B. Woods. *Environmental Disasters*. Minneapolis: Lerner Publications Company, 2008.

INDEX

PHOTO ACKNOWLEDGMENTS

The images in this book are used with the permission of:
© Chris Graythen/Getty Images, pp. 1, 9, and all backgrounds;
U.S. Coast Guard, pp. 2–3; © Transocean/ZUMA Press,
pp. 4–5; © Laura Westlund/Independent Picture Service,
pp. 6, 8 (left), 11, 20; © John Mosier/ZUMA Press, p. 7;
REUTERS/BP/Handout, pp. 8 (right), 12, 13; © Aaron M.
Sprecher/Bloomberg via Getty Images, p. 10; U.S. Air Force
photo by Tech. Sgt. Adrian Cadiz, p. 14; AP Photo/Gerald
Herbert, pp. 15 (left), 21 (left); AP Photo/Charlie Neibergall,
p. 15 (right); AP Photo/Dave Martin, p. 16; U.S. Navy photo by
Mass Communication Specialist 2nd Class Justin Stumberg,
p. 17; AP Photo/Charlie Riedel, p. 18; REUTERS/Lee Celano,
p. 19 (top); AP Photo/Alex Brandon, p. 19 (bottom); © Julie
Dermansky/Photo Researchers, Inc., p. 21 (right); © Erik S.
Lesser/epa/CORBIS, p. 22; AP Photo/Bill Haber, p. 23 (left);
© Win McNamee/Getty Images, p. 23 (right); AP Photo/Gregory
Bull, p. 24; © Todd Strand/Independent Picture Service, pp.
26, 27 (bottom); © Ron Chapple Studios/Dreamstime.com,
p. 27 (top); AP Photo, p. 28 (top); © Bettmann/CORBIS, p. 28
(bottom); AP Photo/John Gaps III, p. 29. Cover photographs
© Win McNamee/Getty Images (pelican); © Chris Graythen/
Getty Images (oil spill); © Charles Ommanney/Getty Images
(beach); NASA/GSFC/METI/ERSDAC/JAROS, and U.S./Japan
ASTER Science Team (jacket flaps).